DOWN TO 'DERRY

DOWN TO 'DERRY:

Coming of Age in Vermont

ISBN Number: 978-1-62646-305-9

This is a memoir. Some names have been changed to protect the identity of those involved.

BookLocker.com, Inc.
2013

First Edition

DOWN TO 'DERRY

Coming of Age in Vermont

A Memoir

Jeanne Heffron Slawson

To Paul and Mark, with
appreciation and love.

To Anne and Kate, with love
from the little girl lucky enough
to become your mother.

As long as the roots are not severed, all is well.
- Being There, 1979

TABLE OF CONTENTS

Prologue

I was born to artists. If they had been true to stereotype, I would have been raised, half-starving, in a garret and led a life of pale but interesting pursuits. Instead, I ended up on Vermont farm, feeding chickens, mucking out stalls, attending a three-room school, and having adventures a girl from the suburbs never dreamed of. This is how it all began:

In the early 1930's, my father taught an evening illustration class at his alma mater, The Boston Museum School of the Fine Arts. My mother was a fashion illustrator taking his class. Soon they were a couple. This evidently didn't sit well with the powers that be, for he was fired. He continued freelancing for The Saturday Evening Post, Pan American Airlines, and American Telephone and Telegraph, among others, until the Boston Post sent him to France and Spain in 1933, where he sketched and painted, submitting his work to the paper. By the time he left for Europe, they were committed; his diary testifies to his pining for the lovely, chestnut-haired woman he'd left behind. When he returned in 1934 they married and, with true artistic spirit, moved to the picturesque city of Taxco, Mexico, to live and paint for a year. They had to return to Massachusetts a little early, however, for the birth of my brother Paul in September 1935. They settled in the suburb of Needham and my father commuted by train to his studio in Boston. I joined the family in June 1938.

I was two when my parents took a driving tour of southern Vermont. My father learned of a derelict house and barn for sale near the small village of South Londonderry, "South 'Derry" to the locals. Surrounded by fourteen acres of hilly fields and woods, the house's only real attraction was its superb view of the West River and Glebe Mountain. Ever an optimist, my father saw possibilities in the sad Cape Cod and sagging barn; the price of $1,400 was manageable. He convinced my mother they should have it.

The dripping pipe in the kitchen was replaced with proper faucets. A Kerosene stove was installed for heating water and cooking. Kerosene lamps were the only source of light after sundown. The two-seater outhouse off the woodshed remained—I always wondered who might share. With these and some minor living space improvements, the house was ready for use by the summer of 1941. Every June for the next six years, the family piled into the Chevy for the hours-long trip to South Londonderry, remaining until just after Labor Day.

In 1946, my parents decided to move permanently the following year. Local professionals were hired to do major remodeling and to add electricity, an indoor bathroom, and two in-floor kerosene heating units. The main feature was the Heatilator, the latest in fireplaces, with multiple vents, one of them being the only source of heat for the second floor. My parents' artistic sensibilities created a warm and attractive house, both efficient and inviting, with a beamed living room ceiling and multi-paned windows, extra large across the back. From living room, dining room, and kitchen we could enjoy the view over the fields down to the river and to the mountain beyond. The house was now white, its black-shuttered windows peering out from under two old maple trees, next to the still-sagging barn. My father's new barn red studio, with its' cathedral ceiling and huge, north-facing window, overlooked the area next to the barn that would later be the paddock; he dreamed of owning horses.

It was June 1947; time to move in. I was nine. I endured one more tortuous ride from Needham, the trip punctuated by my brothers' cries of, "She's gonna be sick again!"

My parents had thought of everything. My father could mail his work to his publisher, making a few trips to Boston for meetings. His gregarious nature was satisfied by outings to the village and serving as a town selectman. My mother retired before Mark's birth in 1941 and didn't resume her career until Paul was fifteen. The quiet life suited her reserved nature. She made our house and gardens lovely—and kept the family going. Get-togethers with a few other transplanted families comprised my parents' social life.

For me, life took on a new vitality and color. We had our own horses. Over time, we acquired a ram, a goat, a cat, various dogs, ducks, geese, chickens, and two black-eared lambs. Our schoolhouse had three rooms—

an early "open school," where we learned a great deal more than the Three R's.

During the summer, our mother's lists of chores for us appeared on the kitchen bulletin board each morning. I got the "girl's" jobs: *clean bathroom, ring and hang out wash, iron Daddy's underwear,* and so on, as well as my usual chores of setting the supper table, making salads, and drying dishes. Animal care was a given. We earned our allowance of twenty-five cents a week. Our father now commuted on foot to his studio, where he created schoolbook illustrations, coming back to the house for lunch at noon. Badminton was the after-dinner game in the summer, Ping-Pong in the winter. Winter weekends we skied at Bromley Mountain. My brothers were good. I was cold.

My Vermont memories are vivid still. With these small stories, I've tried to capture many of them—nostalgic, humorous, even painful—from 1947 to 1952, the five years before our rural adventure came to an unexpected end.

Down to 'Derry

The Little Red Squeak's engine roared. The bleached red pickup my father named was backing out of its space near his studio. He bought the ancient, noisy Ford to carry lumber, feed for the animals, anything large. During mud season in April, wallowing up to its hubcaps, it was the only way to get in and out of our dirt lane. On that particular summer day he was going down to the village.

"Can I go?" The screen door slammed behind me as I sprinted for the truck. In a place where the nearest neighbors were a retired couple down the lane and three bachelor brothers in the farmhouse out on the main road, downtown South Londonderry beckoned like Broadway. If we were fast enough, all three of us kids would go.

We hopped into the back of the pickup. Bucketing along to the end of our rocky lane and out onto the washboard main road, we passed Tuttle's farm, waving to the brother who hauled and chopped wood day in and day out.

"Hi Phil!"

He waved back, calling out a cheerful grunt. My brother Mark practiced for his future as a college gymnast by crawling out of the truck bed and lowering himself onto the running board, crouching against the fender and hanging onto the lip of the bed. Fortunately for him, my father didn't see that. Sometimes Mark and Paul sat on the tailgate, swinging their feet. Throwing pebbles at signs was entertaining, until one ricocheted and hit the driver's side door.

"Cut that out!"

Traveling past Holsteins grazing in the Tuttle's pasture or staring at us as they chewed their cuds, the Squeak executed several downhill runs with sharp turns. Soon the West River came into view below, winding toward town. Huge trees lined the banks; underbrush hung low over the slow-moving water, rocks jutting out here and there. In the summer, the river meandered; in the spring it raged. About a mile further along, up on the right, was the Clough's clapboard house. Old Jim Clough sat on the front porch every summer, his gaze fixed on his barn across the road. It sank further toward the water after every spring flood. When it finally floated away, he retired into the house and died. With the Stone Steps Restaurant in sight, we were almost there. Next left turn after the dam.

As the river approached the big dam, it was deep. Flowing over the dam, it looked like dark molten glass, falling heavily to roaring foam. The bridge crossed to the Square and Main Street. On the left at the opposite end was Taylor's Mill, its huge water wheel turning. My father once asked a worker what they made. "Oh, inza-outzas an' whirla-whirla's," he replied. The mill made turned wood pieces.

Our first stop, on The Square across from the mill and just below steep Church Hill, was Landman's Hardware and Variety. Caspar "Cap" Landman was a genial man in engineer's cap and overalls; his grandfather founded the store in the 1800s. My father enjoyed chewing the fat, as he called it, with Cap and often bought hammers, saws, and such things as ten-penny nails. I always made a beeline for the toy section where I found tiny plastic baby dolls in miniscule diapers, with bottles and pastel flannel blankets. My brothers headed for the comic section. I liked that too. "Archie" was my favorite, with Betty, Veronica, and Jughead. Our father usually bought us some small thing. He enjoyed our outings as much as we did, his illustration assignments requiring much solitude.

Having completed our business there, and not needing the services of Marvin Howard's home-based funeral parlor in The Brick House on the corner, we rode down Main Street to the Post Office, behind Elmer's Market. There, Ora Slade, Postmaster and fun-loving tease, held forth. "Orie" was a big man with slicked-back hair and a bristling mustache that emphasized his large teeth.

"Well, look who's heah!"

With a wicked grin, he began to josh me about my nonexistent boyfriends. Polly Johnson, his assistant, always joined in the fun. Her benevolent good nature overcame prominent teeth and double chins. Formerly chief operator at the telephone exchange on Melendy Hill, and therefore fount of all information, she had a place of honor in the community. Though it took only two minutes to check our mailbox, we never got out of the post office quickly. Chatting and being teased were too much fun.

We made a quick stop next door at Elmer's Market to pick up Pepperidge Farm White, imported at my mother's request, then retraced our route, past the riverside Champion Fire Company No. 5, across the bridge, and left down the dip to the Green Mountain Farmers Cooperative Exchange, Inc. The brick-red building was long. It had to be, to accommodate its name. We were greeted by Curtis Shattuck, the proprietor, who had glasses that twinkled and a smile to match.

"You might want to see the kittens. Got some new ones."

I shivered with anticipation. He and my father went into the office, my brothers and I into the feed storage room. In the hazy, mote-laden light from the loading door, we scaled mountains of burlap, our nostrils filling with the pungent smell of oats, corn, and other grains. There were kittens all right, some frolicking, some hiding, all cute. Mom said if we could find one guaranteed not to grow any bigger, we could bring it home. When Daddy and Mr. Shattuck had settled the town's affairs, completed the day's order, and moved heavy feedbags off the loading platform into the back of the truck, we headed for home, wedged among the scratchy mounds.

It was back to the bucolic life, until next time the Squeak roared its call to town.

Winning Isn't Anything

After a summer of competing in horse shows as part of a riding club, my brother Paul and I, eleven and nine, won the state's top prizes for horsemanship for children eighteen and under—a family sweep—which should have brought excitement and joy. Instead, it brought me admonition and guilt. I had made a mistake. I had beaten my older brother.

All summer Paul and I trained at the Chester Riding Club. The week before horse shows we took individual riding lessons in the dusty outdoor ring. Sometimes my face was tear-streaked from exhaustion and from hearing my instructor shout, "Do that figure eight again! I want a two-second lead change!" or whatever it was that day. The days were hot, the work hard, and I loved it. I felt an affinity with horses and was said to have "a good seat" and "good hands." And it was the only sport I could fully engage in, having been born with an imperfect heart.

For horse shows, I wore long jodhpurs, a white shirt, the red corduroy vest my mother made, a red tie, and saddle shoes. My mother curled my hair with bobby pins. Jackets and riding boots were too expensive. I envied the other girls in their snappy jackets and shiny boots, especially one girl, the daughter of a horse farm owner and show judge. She had grown up in the horse world, had all the trappings money could buy, and was used to winning.

Dana had her own horse. He was so beautifully trained he could have competed by himself—except that in equitation classes, it is the rider who is judged. While she had the advantage of always riding the same horse, I rotated among several club horses. Every time I saw her, appearing aloof and sure of herself with her red hair and perfect outfit, astride her perfect red horse, I felt myself shrink a little. But as I executed the judge's commands, I felt my confidence return. To their credit, judges didn't appear to favor beautiful riding togs over homemade vests and saddle shoes.

The summer passed and the race for ribbons grew close. It seemed that every time I won a blue, Dana or Paul would win the next. If Paul felt competitive with me, he didn't show it. Skiing was his sport. It was my first year of showing and I wasn't aware of the accumulation of points or an award at the end of the season. All I knew was that winning blue ribbons was good. At the end of the season, when the points were added up and the results announced, I had won and Paul, with only two fewer points, came in second. I was surprised—and thrilled. I would soon learn to stifle that.

Maybe our parents wanted to protect Paul's feelings and didn't want me to get a "swelled head," but they really didn't celebrate our wins. I could tell my father was proud, but my mother repeatedly coached me, "When they congratulate you, be sure to tell them that your brother came in only two points behind," as if I'd done something underhanded that required explanation. So I dutifully repeated her words every time anyone offered congratulations, feeling the sand of my self-esteem run out onto the floor.

The awards banquet took place that fall at a hotel in White River Junction. It was the crowning event of the horse show season. We had to make a long drive and stay overnight in a hotel. My mother had made me a new red wool jumper, which I wore with a white, puff-sleeved blouse, white socks and Mary Janes. As we got ready to go to the banquet, my mother took me aside to coach me one last time. When I was called up to the podium, I shook the man's hand, thanked him, then mouthed the obligatory words, as if my mother were standing right there. Back in my seat at the banquet table, I looked at my prize. Underneath the proud brass horse the plaque read, "Vermont State Champion, 1947, Junior Horsemanship, Jean Heffron." My first name was spelled wrong. It wasn't me. I felt even more inconsequential. Then Paul was called up to receive his Reserve Champion ribbon, I'm sure without having been given a mantra to recite.

After we got home the next day, I don't remember the awards being mentioned again. It was like some fairy tale I'd heard—but the proof sat on my bureau, solid and shiny. As I stroked its beautiful outlines, I was proud. Despite the admonitions and the misspelling, I had won—we both had won.

Off to Superior School

September used to be the time for the major pack-up before our return to Massachusetts for the winter, but the year before we moved was different. We stayed on for three months, so Paul and I could attend sixth and third grade at Central Elementary School. At the end of that time, my parents hoped to know if we could be adequately educated there. I cared nothing about the quality of instruction. I cared a lot about whether the kids would like me. To the locals, "summer people" meant, at worst, rich, snooty, and foreign, and at best, temporary and unimportant.

As the first day of school approached, I agonized about what might make me more interesting. Not my horseback riding—to them, a rich man's pastime—not Roger, my blond first-grade love in Massachusetts. If they found out his mother put cold cream on his face before we went sledding, they'd laugh themselves silly. So no horses, no Roger. What? I couldn't share farm stories because my parents were artists, and in South 'Derry, being a painter meant having a bad day if it rained. I busied myself with silent worries while my mother busied herself making a red and blue plaid dress with puff sleeves and a white collar for me to wear the first day. If love could be measured by adorable outfits, I was loved.

Daddy drove Paul and me that morning. Mark didn't go because there was no kindergarten. The car was quiet, each of us in our own thoughts. Just past the library, we turned up the lane leading to the school. Crowning the top of the hill was the spanking white clapboard building, its just-washed windows staring black and cool, taking stock of nervous children who had rehearsed their opening day lines. I clutched my school bag as if new pencils and a spiral notebook could transmit courage. As we pulled up, gray cement stairs loomed, rising steeply toward a big black door. I thought briefly of begging to go back home.

Paul led the way up the steps. "Welcome to Central Elementary!" said a smiling woman at the top, whom I would later know as Miss Phyllis Johnson. Her tea-cozy comfortableness lifted my faint spirits, but my hope that she would be my teacher was dashed when she sent me across the hall and Paul further on. With a little wave, he went off.

"Hi!" "Hi!" "That new? "Mine too." The chatter bounced off the walls, making even louder the sounds of familiarity, of belonging, sounds that didn't include me. My new red lace-ups moved me to the classroom door. Glancing about, I took in the controlled chaos of kids finding seats, raising desktops, and dumping supplies. Then my red shoes froze to the floor. Standing at the front of the room, the tips of her long, spidery fingers pressed on the desktop, her lips like two thin slices of baloney, was my new teacher, Mrs. Elva Purcell. Hanging from her gaunt frame and beef jerky arms was a shapeless creation in dead flounder gray. Either Halloween was early or I was in trouble.

"Name?" Her voice snapped like a whip. I mumbled it. "Over there, second row from the window, behind Samuel." Samuel? I didn't know anyone, much less Samuel. She pointed, a boy held up a hesitant hand, and I walked to my seat, examining the floor to avoid curious stares. My ideas for opening lines flew from my head. As others came in and were given seat assignments, I turned slightly to see who was around me. "Hi, I'm Gracie," said a smiling, dark-haired girl with bangs. "This is Jack." I swung around to meet him. Dull eyes stared back, their pale color reminding me of the aggies in my brother's marble bag. His face was sallow, the skin drawn over sunken cheeks, mouth open. His nose ran. I wanted to offer a Kleenex, but thought better of it. Jack returned my greeting with a slight nod. My gaze wandered to the other side of the room. One particularly tall, big-boned boy could barely wedge himself into the small chair attached to his desk. He glowered, his lower lip protruding as if he were ready for a fight. "That's Ethan," Gracie told me, "He's been held back a lot."

I didn't raise my hand that day. As Mrs. Purcell began our lessons, I watched much as one would watch a coiled snake.

Mrs. Purcell, with her tight gray bun, pinched mouth, and wire-rimmed glasses, could "lace into you pretty good," as my classmates put it. Within weeks, I found my wariness was not misplaced.

"I will not chew gum in class, I will not chew gum in class, I will not chew gum in class..." One hundred times.

My pencil moved down the yellow lined page, my teeth and fingers clenched as I wrote my sentence, that sentence having been meted out by Mrs. Purcell.

"Honestly, I wasn't, I was just chewing the inside of my mouth," I responded when accused. That got a "likely story" look, and I was sent back to complete my sentence. As I handed her the pages, her lips pursed with satisfaction.

"I hope this will teach you a lesson." It did. It taught me that sometimes the truth won't set you free.

I finished third grade in Massachusetts. After our move, I returned to Central Elementary in September. Mrs. Purcell, who would have been my teacher for two more years, had resigned or been fired, so I began fourth grade with a clean slate. Having already survived the worst of being new, I slipped back into the school's routine with less anxiety. By the time the snow was in six-foot drifts by the roadside, I felt quite comfortable.

The sweet smell of oats lingered in my nose. The horses were fed and so were my brothers and I—oats too, but soft and hot, with raisins and brown sugar. Wool jackets buttoned up, earflaps down, boots and mittens on, we were ready to catch our ride to school. Before we began the quarter-mile walk to the end of the lane, Mom took pieces of soapstone from the warm oven and slipped them into our mittens. It was below freezing again.

We stepped onto the porch, our goodbyes steaming in the frigid air. The plow had come through yesterday, so our boots squeaked on the hard-packed snow as we trudged along. Waiting next to the main road, I did a little dance to keep my feet warm. Finally, the green Jeep crunched to a stop next to the snow bank. It served as a school bus for the five of us who lived too close to take the real one but too far to walk. I crossed my fingers, hoping I'd get to sit on Harold's lap again. He was older, and very handsome. His parents came from Oyster Bay la-de-da, Long Island, but moved to Vermont for his father's health and now raised Holsteins up on Middletown Road.

The door to the Jeep swung open. Orie, providing this private "bus" service at the time, flashed a welcoming smile as he asked the almost-daily question:

"Didja bring me some cupcakes? I'm awful hungry."

Orie was also a decorated veteran of The War. Even though his shoulder had been shattered, his good nature was intact. I often brought him chocolate cupcakes, made from the recipe in my cookbook with the perfect little girl on the cover.

"No, not today—but tomorrow, okay?"

"Awww...promise?"

We piled in, and my wish came true. I perched happily on Harold's lap. The week before, as we were getting settled, his thumbnail had scratched my forehead. I was almost sorry when the scab fell off.

We were the last pickup, so Central Elementary School soon came into view. The ground sloped away from it, leading to the playground and a field where the town trucks were parked.

"Bye, Orie, see you thisafta!"

We climbed the steep steps, hung our coats in the hall, lined up our boots, and went to our rooms and our desks. We sat down, then stood up again.

"I pledge allegiance...."

The morning's lessons began with the third grade, nearest the window, then went on to the fourth and fifth, right across the room. Occasional eavesdropping helped with catching up or getting ahead. The school's one hundred students were divided among three large rooms—grades one and two, three through five, and six through eight. A plaque by the front door proclaimed that the State found our school "Superior," rather than the usual "Standard," perhaps because of the library, extracurricular options, and the innovative hot lunch program. No doubt the mayhem was not a factor.

Miss Gertrude Peckenham, our good-natured fourth grade teacher, could also be strict. A rangy woman of about six feet, her ropey arms ended in no-nonsense hands with long fingers. Those fingers had twisted many a lug wrench when she was a mechanic in the Marines. Now they wrote on the blackboard, corrected papers, and applied the occasional Band-Aid. Her dark hair was parted in the middle and caught in a bun at the nape of her neck. A gap interrupted her broad, red-lipsticked smile.

It looked like it was going to be another normal day. I listened to lessons, sweated over math, went out for recess and to the basement for lunch. Feeling sleepy after lunch, I was halfheartedly doing some written work when I was startled by a disturbance a couple of rows over. Ethan, now a fifth grader, was at it again. Miss Peckenham spoke sternly to him. Most of us would have quieted, but not Ethan. He stood up.

"You can't make me!"

Ethan was often angry. I think I would have been too if I were fourteen and still in fifth grade. Miss Peckenham's face flushed. Scowling, she stood up and in about four long strides was at Ethan's desk. They glared at each other. It was hard to say whose face was redder.

"I'll teach you to sass me!"

She raised her hand, now a fist, and punched him, hard, in the face. My mouth fell open. Ethan fell to the floor, howling. Wrapping those powerful fingers around his ankle, she began to drag him out of the room. Just as Ethan was sliding out the door, he grabbed the leg of our prized RCA Victrola. On casters, it rolled along, wobbling and bumping—Miss Peckenham, Ethan, and His Master's Voice, all headed for the principal's office. Ethan was still howling. The rest of us looked at each other in silence—we knew what awaited him. Although twinkly, ample Viola Winfield's mantra was *I will not tolerate fisticuffs,* as Principal, she believed that a few whacks with a length of garden hose were appropriate punishment.

Within half an hour, Ethan slouched back into the room, holding his arm, his face still red. He remained quiet the rest of the day.

Winter's early dusk began to fall. The sound of the school bus toiling up the hill to the front door was followed by the hum of Orie's jeep pulling up behind it. The day ended as it began, orderly and routine. Students packed up belongings, bid Miss Peckenham goodbye, and shuffled to the hall to don coats and boots.

I imagined telling my parents about Ethan. Although my father sometimes showed his temper, he was never violent and would "raise Cain," as my mother put it, if he knew. Perhaps I wouldn't be allowed to come back. Being a relative newcomer, I was anxious not to cause trouble. I decided to keep quiet. Ethan dropped out of school and there were no more incidents like that—not right away.

I was in the seventh grade. Mrs. Winfield had left and we had a new principal. A tiny woman with a tight brown perm, enormous tortoise-shell glasses, and a red mouth slash, Olive Banker was a fine teacher who founded the chorus and encouraged us to be creative. She was popular with students, but she brooked no nonsense. One afternoon Larry, another boy who had been held back, responded to a warning by leaping up and shouting. Without hesitation, she strode up to him and smacked his face with the back of her hand, the hand with the enormous gold and amber ring I often admired. Part of a tooth flew to the floor. Blubbering, Larry was sent home. Mrs. Banker had discontinued the hose, but this was hardly an improvement. Larry's parents were furious and sent him back to school—with the note of apology they made him write. Mrs. Banker read it, nodded toward his seat, and Larry was back in class.

One day in late spring, Patty, a classmate and friend, invited me home to play and have dinner. She lived with her grandparents, mother, and brother Mickey, just beyond the Stone Steps Restaurant, an easy walk from school.

As we neared the house, I waved to her grandfather sitting in his rocker on the front porch and, as usual, staring at his collapsing barn at the river's edge. Patty's grandmother, birdlike and busy, bustled through the screen door.

"Hi there, Jeanne. You like chicken? I'm going to fix a nice one for dinner."

"Yes, thank you."

Then I saw the axe. Before her intention could really register, she grabbed a chicken from the flock pecking around the yard, threw it over a nearby stump, and, with one swing, sent its head flying. Yes, they do run around like... I was horrified but fascinated. I don't know why I didn't scream. Then I thought of Ethan and Larry and their treatment at school. At least the chicken didn't suffer, and instinct told me this violence was justified.

No Don Ho

If he played it one more time, I'd strangle him.

Younger brother Mark's favorite gift for his seventh birthday was a ukulele. He practiced diligently, but one song, only one song, *Red River Valley.* Constantly playing in my head, either truly or in memory, was the last line, "I'll remember the Red River VAL-ley, and the cowboy who loved me so truuue." We were all sick of it.

I was in the kitchen with Mom, making Mickey Mouse Salads for dinner (a canned pear half on lettuce, dates for ears, raisins for eyes, and a maraschino cherry for the nose), when we heard wailing. It got closer, and louder. Mark appeared, his face tomato-red, tears streaming. He was clutching his precious ukulele, or what remained of it. It was now just jagged strips of polished wood, strings broken and springing in all directions. Between tears and hiccups, he said he had gone to the barn to play for the horses—no doubt due to a lack of appreciation by humans. All three of our horses were exceptionally sweet natured, so Mark didn't hesitate to enter Ceci's box stall and begin his serenade. Yes, that song. Maybe horses just don't appreciate music, or at least country music, because she turned her back. When this failed to bring peace, she delivered her review with a perfectly placed kick, shattering Mark's musical dreams. As we stared at him and his destroyed instrument, he cried out in amazement and outrage.

"She kicked me in the *ukulele*!"

Smart horse.

A Very Small Outing

The thermos snapped into the top of my blue lunchbox. Now that we had hot lunch at school, I only used my lunchbox in the summer. That day I was going on a picnic by myself, as I sometimes did when the boys went off with Daddy.

Mom packed a peanut butter and marshmallow fluff sandwich, a peach, and two Oreo cookies. She always made vanilla milk, my favorite. I let the screen door bang behind me and headed off down the dirt road my mother named Derry Lane. There were only two houses on the lane, ours being number One.

Going by the pasture gate and the salt lick, I went up the small rise past my father's studio, scuffing pebbles with my blue Keds. I passed the huge maple tree with the sandbox underneath, by then used for making tracks for my brothers' miniature racing cars.

Soon I came to my rock, off to the right by the stone pasture wall. It was huge and surrounded by gigantic ferns. I waded through the weeds in the ditch—no Skunk Cabbage now, to make me hold my nose—pushed through the thick ferns, and found little footholds to get to the top of the boulder. It wasn't easy with my lunchbox in one hand. I sat down and arranged my lunch with care. If something fell off, I'd never find it. When everything was ready, I looked out beyond that huge maple tree to the field where our horses were grazing, and over toward the Tuttle's farm. I couldn't see their old farmhouse and gray barn from there. Glebe Mountain sat bluish in the distance, clouds drifting over, going nowhere. I could see all the way down the valley to the spire on Church Hill, downtown.

I looked down into the green jungle below and saw little blossoms, orange with rusty spots, poking up through the ferns. If I squeezed them, they popped, the seeds scattering to make more plants next year. I leaned over to take a closer look at the patches of gray lichen on my lumpy picnic table. When I got very close, I saw that they were really thousands of tiny cups. I wondered how they could be so small and still not be hurt when I stepped on them.

I poured the vanilla milk into the thermos top and sipped. I ate very slowly. Each bite was the best. Peach juice dripped down my chin. At last I pulled the Oreos apart, licking off the frosting, then slowly eating the cookies, savoring the taste of chocolate.

The cows on the other side of the stone wall were having a picnic too. Their all-day munching made milk for George and Foster Tuttle's evening chore. Their brother Phil didn't do any milking. They said he was "simple," so his job was to split the wood for the winter's fires. He always seemed happy, though. Thirty-five cows took a long time to milk every morning and night, but the family's living depended on milk—that and maple syrup. I hoped when sugaring season came next March we'd get to ride again on the pung, the big sled pulled by their draft horses, carrying dozens of buckets from the maples to the sugar house. There we'd watch the sugaring-off process, boiling the sap down in huge vats until it became syrup. Then one of the Tuttle brothers would give us spoons to make "sugar-on-snow" by pouring hot syrup over fresh snow—instant candy.

Now I gazed up at the clouds, by then looking like the tops of lemon meringue pies. It wasn't really hot and there was a little breeze. The cows weren't lying down, so no rain that day.

I cleared my rock table, clicked the thermos into place, and snapped the silver latch. Clutching the handle and sliding down, I landed over my head in ferns. I pushed through the undergrowth and turned toward home, swinging my blue lunchbox, knowing I'd be back soon.

A Summer Snowdrop

"Get that animal out of my living room!"

Mom had lost her usual equanimity, protesting loudly as the rest of us—Daddy, Paul, Mark, and I—tried to corral our newest adoptee. The small goat was one of the castoffs my father brought home, more attractive than some of the others. Ramsey, our ram, was big and ugly, but had won our hearts; the six milk goats didn't last long because no one wanted to milk them. This little animal, however, was delight itself, a tiny creature, spotless white, with an elfin air. Her delicate legs, with their tiny patent leather hooves, carried a small round body, a flip of a tail, and a small head that was mostly large yellow eyes and drooping ears. Two adorable little dewlaps under her chin swung with every movement.

My brothers and I were thrilled. My mother was skeptical, but patient—at first. The goat was so young that we brought her into the kitchen for her bowl of milk. She dropped delicately to her knees and sipped, while we watched, entranced.

"Isn't she cute? She's so small and so white! Let's call her Snowdrop, like those little spring flowers!"

She lifted her little head. She watched. After a few seconds, she gathered her legs under her and bolted toward the living room. We scrambled to catch up.

Glancing about, she apparently saw peaks to be scaled. She launched herself onto the sofa, springing from there onto the big Windsor chair, and finally onto my father's favorite reading chair by the fireplace, scaling it to the top of the back cushion. From there she surveyed the landscape. Everyone was laughing—everyone except my mother. Her face reddened as she saw livestock careening around on her prized custom slipcovers.

"I won't have it!"

She went to the kitchen and returned with a broom raised high. She meant business.

"Now, Connie, take it easy," cajoled my father.

"I paid good money to have Mr. Schorch make those slipcovers, and I'll be darned if some goat is going to ruin them!"

Meanwhile, my brothers and I were falling all over each other, trying to grab Snowdrop, but she was too quick.

The front door stood open, and Snowdrop saw her chance to make an exit before that lady with the red face could get close enough to make things unpleasant. Her hooves skittered across the braided rug and clattered across the pine floor until, with a flip of that tail, she bounded through the doorway into the front yard.

"That's the last time an animal will eat in my kitchen!"

And it was.

A Timeless Legacy

Sunday. Morning sun flooded the windows at the end of the living room; the pine table glowed. The fire, banked all night, was stoked and starting to crackle, smoldering wood smells rising. Still in my nightgown, I sat on the sofa, warm Muffin purring in my lap.

My father turned away from the fire. He wore his favorite hound's-tooth-check wool shirt, dungarees, and the leather belt with the square, hammered-silver buckle, bought when he and my mother lived in Mexico.

Moving toward the wall between the windows, he reached up to the antique banjo clock, an auction find of some years before. It was a handsome thing, mahogany with brass knobs and trim, a tracery of a soft blue and gold design on the center panel, a graceful finial on top. He pulled the rounded glass cover away from the face and adjusted the black metal hands. Through the clear, gold-bordered rectangle in the middle of the black glass door at the bottom, I could see the big brass pendulum. He opened the door and reached in to take out the stubby metal key. Inserting it into the keyhole on the clock face, he slowly wound it twelve times, exactly twelve times, never more, never less. He said that's what kept it accurate—not winding the steel coil too tight. The pendulum's rhythmic cadence assured me that all was well.

Later, the clock was stored away. I didn't see it for many years, but didn't forget it. I told my mother it was the only thing I really wanted to inherit. I didn't have to wait that long, as she kindly gave it to me when my husband and I moved into our first house. In every house since, it has said, "Home."

Now I wind it every Sunday, exactly twelve times. The pendulum resumes its steady beat. I think of that little girl, so sure of a safe and predictable world.

Dora Takes the Plunge

I looked at my feet. They were white. Snowdrop, our pet goat, wasn't that white. My eyes moved up my grasshopper-thin legs to knees that knocked like the castanets my parents got in Mexico. Goose bumps rose from my purple-mottled flesh. My lips, as blue as my bathing suit, grimaced over chattering teeth.

It was another day of nine o' clock swimming lessons at Hapgood Pond. Stretching across to the woods far beyond, it was fed by mountain springs. Our instructor was a college student named Wendy whose summer job was torturing children by making them flail around in freezing water. She seemed to love her work. Standing on the man-made beach, fully dressed, including a sweater, she smiled and shouted directions at her little victims. Shrieks, gasps, and cries of "It's not fair!" moved her not at all.

"You're doing fine! Stroke, stroke!" Her smile was infuriating.

That morning Wendy directed us to walk over to the dock, where there was a diving board. Our progress had been good, and she pronounced us ready to try swimming in deep water. I was panicky, because in deep water there was no chance of surreptitiously touching bottom with a big toe, as I had been doing to hide my shortness of breath.

"I want you to jump off the dock or the board and swim out to the rope."

That rope seemed miles away but was probably only about ten or fifteen yards. Hiding our fear with a chorus of whining, we headed for the dock and threw down our towels. A couple of the boys, in a burst of derring-do, ran to the board where, *oh-eee-oh-eee-oh-ing* like Tarzan, they leapt out over the water. We stragglers followed, jumping one-by-one to our frigid fate. But one of us had come up with a plan.

Dora, a robust girl with more natural padding than common sense, had figured out how to outwit Wendy and at the same time avoid refrigeration. Her reasoning may have been, *If my sweater keeps me warm, why take it off?*

Before anyone realized what she was doing, a geyser erupted as Dora and her Shaker-knit hit the water. In no time, they were going under. We were about to learn how to drown. The rest of us, useless at rescue but excellent at screaming, did our best. Wendy was left with no choice but to jump in too. She had time to throw off only her sweater and shoes before diving in and Australian-crawling to the rescue. She quickly reached Dora who, surfacing briefly, wrapped around her like an octopus. Wendy pushed her off, put her in a lifeguard's chokehold, and dragged her and her hundred-pound knitwear back to shore, depositing her onto the grass.

With Dora laid out like a landed salmon, gasping but clearly alive, the rest of us climbed out and wrapped our quaking bodies with towels. We looked at each other, then at Wendy. Our stiff little lips broke into smiles. Seeing Wendy shivering, miserable, and blue-lipped too, we snickered, then giggled, then laughed out loud. Oh, sweet revenge. It almost made the weeks of water torture worth it. That there were no drownings proved they had also been successful, but that was incidental.

A Sheepish Tale

"You better watch out. You'll be sorry."

My little brother, Mark, was teasing Ramsey, our pet ram, again. He rubbed his horn stumps, making Ramsey want to butt—but Mark avoided that by moving just beyond the length of the tether. I hoped for a day of reckoning.

A dim bulb. That best described Ramsey, a sorry, unwanted beast my father took pity on and brought home. He was big and rawboned, with a stringy white coat and large, topaz eyes pierced by black, evil-looking slits. Sawed-off horns left little stumps between the banana peel ears drooping on either side of his Roman-nosed head. His hooves were cloven and sharp. Anything in his path was haute cuisine, so was he roped to a stake most of the day, only grass on the menu. He was as dumb as the post he was tied to. When he was off his tether and heard his name called, a few seconds passed before it registered. Then he'd raise his head, chewing as he swiveled his yellow gaze. Then, with a delighted kick of his heels, he would take off toward the caller, fast, running *right by*, to stop within a few feet and look around with a "Where did everybody go?" air. We hooted at his stupidity.

"Help! Help! Waaa!" The piteous wails came from the barn one day. Running, Daddy and I found Mark splayed against the wall of an empty box stall, with Ramsey bouncing him against it like a tennis ball. Ramsey was obviously enjoying himself, and our arrival didn't stop him for a second. Grabbing his collar, my father hauled him off. I was relieved to see my little brother rescued, but I couldn't help savoring the delicious moment my dire forecast came true.

After that incident, we realized how seriously that powerful animal could have hurt Mark and appreciated Ramsey's restraint in choosing such a limited horns-on approach to press his point. Sheepishly, we had to admit that within that dim bulb lurked a glimmer of thought—and forbearance.

Pride

Pride goeth before a fall, they say. That day the proud one didn't take the fall.

My father and I drove to Chester, and soon pulled into the circular drive and up to the big white barn with the sign reading *Buttonwood Farm*. Here I had learned to ride under the tutelage of the kind and distinguished Ivan Taylor, known as Ivy. His teaching helped me win my unsung award the year before. Then the riding school was sold and was now under the direction of Johnny-somebody from New York.

My father cut the engine and pulled the brake. We sat for a few moments, gazing at the familiar building. So many happy memories here: my first lessons at seven on Jo-Jo, a sleek Welsh pony; all-day trail rides, sometimes following the hunt; my quasi-boyfriend, Peter, with his blue eyes and sandy hair; the days of hot, sweaty practice in the ring, preparing for horse shows.

The place didn't beckon now. Ivy had taken his students up the road to a smaller stable. My father decided I should stay with the more upscale stable, no doubt seeing more trophies in my future.

We went into the small front office and found no one. I felt guilty even being there, betraying Ivy. After a short wait, my father called out, and from the tack room beyond emerged a burly man with a tousle of red hair, carrying a bridle. He thrust out his hand.

"Hello there. I'm Tommy Kelly. I mind the horses here." His Irish accent complemented his welcoming smile.

"I'm Walt Heffron. This is my daughter, Jeanne."

We shook hands. Then an excess of fatherly pride laid the groundwork for trouble.

"She won the Vermont junior championship last year."

"Did she now?" Tommy grinned at me. "That's quite something for a bit of thing like you. And how old were you?"

"Nine," I said and fell back into silence.

"And it was for kids eighteen and under," added my father.

"Most impressive. And you're lookin' for a ride today?

Ordinarily at a new stable the first ride would include the supervision of a lesson. I looked at my father, to see if he approved. He nodded. I nodded.

"Then come with me, I've got just the mount for you," he said with a mischievous grin.

We followed him into the familiar stable, its spacious stalls now filled with unknown horses—but horses are horses and I perked up. Tommy strode down the corridor, opened a stall door, and disappeared momentarily. He came out leading a black horse big enough to single-handedly pull the Budweiser beer wagon.

"This here's Midnight. She's a real nice ride when you get the feel of her. She hasn't been out yet this spring, so she might be a bit frisky, but since you're a champ you won't have any trouble, I'm sure."

My father beamed, patting me reassuringly on the shoulder.

"She's got what it takes," he said.

Tommy saddled her and led her outside, where he cupped his hands and gave me a leg up. So far, she was docile. He gestured as he looked up at me.

"Will you look at 'er up there—no bigger than a bag o' peanuts."

I'm sure a bag of peanuts would have felt more secure. At under five feet and sixty pounds dripping-wet, I was to control a horse five-feet-four at the withers, and probably thirteen hundred pounds. My legs were too short to even begin to wrap around the animal; the stirrups had to be set at maximum height. I didn't have a good feeling about this. I was accustomed to riding far smaller horses, on which the chances of influencing behavior were at least better. I looked at my father, who was still beaming. He was counting on me.

Taking up the reins, I flicked them and clucked softly, giving Midnight the signal to move ahead. She immediately flexed her neck, biting down on the bit and taking small, sideways steps, hooves lifting smartly. She was clearly thrilled to be out of the stall. I could feel the tremendous power in those muscles as she danced along.

"Ah, she's feelin' good today, isn't she?" said Tommy, as he and my father walked alongside. She might have been. I, however, was feeling distinctly apprehensive, but had something to prove. We reached the riding ring, where the two men accompanied me through the gate.

"Now, darlin', just walk her around once or twice and then we'll have a little trot."

We? He was safely unmounted, his battered leather boots on terra firma.

Midnight didn't have a mind to walk. To jog, yes, to prance, to skitter sideways, yes. My splayed legs could do nothing to control her, my supposedly "good" hands just an annoyance, as she tasted freedom.

After several dancing turns around the ring, Tommy called out,

"Now let's try a bit of a trot, shall we?"

I would have been happy to give him the opportunity. I tightened my grip on the already taut reins and reluctantly gave Midnight the leg signal to trot—or tried to—my legs hardly touched her sides, so had little effect. Well, some effect. They irritated her. She translated my signal into *buck* and did. She lowered her head and arched her back as she propelled herself up, flinging her heels in the air for the finishing touch. Once, twice, three times. I hung on. Then with a mighty heave, she outdid herself and I went off. It seemed I was falling forever, flying through the air like that bag of peanuts. I landed on my back, my bare head punching a dent in the spring mud.

I couldn't breathe. I didn't cry. Real riders don't cry. Tommy and my father ran from their places at the rail.

"Ah, there you go, darlin'" said Tommy as he pulled me to my feet. I was gasping, but at least I was breathing again.

"There now," said my father as he brushed me off. Turning to Tommy, he said, "She's a little out of practice—the winter, you know.

She'll be fine, won't you, Jeannie." It was if it were a little bump I'd taken and now all was well.

There was no question about whether I would remount. All true riders get right back on. Not to would be admitting the horse won and being forever afraid. Even I didn't question it, though looking up at her massive black bulk, it crossed my mind.

I was launched back into the saddle and took up the reins just so, snaffle rein between thumb and forefinger, curb rein running between my third and pinky fingers. Surely those hands could best a dumb animal's scheming. Except horses aren't dumb. They sense any fear or tension in the rider and, if they are of a certain turn of mind, use that opportunity to try to take charge.

We began again. A walk, no, dance, then the signal to trot. Gathering her legs under her, she again flung herself up, this time adding a sideways twist, with the heel flip for a finish. Repeat. Soon I was airborne again. As I lay in the mud with pancake lungs, I thought *at least I won't have to get back on this time.*

Again the *there-you-go*'s and the *there now*'s, the wiping off of dark slime, the cupped hands to relaunch me. *They can't be doing this.* My mind screamed *No*, but was stilled by male authority and the remaining shreds of my ego; after all, I was supposed to be a champion. I let those two put me back onto that spring-fever-crazed animal and send me off with a pat.

The rest was a given. More dancing, skittering, bucking, and contortions, more airborne bag of peanuts, more head in the mud. At least I didn't land face down. I lay still, trying to pull in air, tears at last falling.

"Well, darlin', I guess old Midnight needs a bit o' fresh air on her own before we try again."

Yeah, I guess. And try again? I'd kill myself first. Better than having it done for me.

In chess, the pawn is the piece with the smallest size and value. I was the pawn that day, used in a game between a proud father and a cocky Irishman.

Corky Goes Down

Our young stallion, Corky, was so named because he almost bounced rather than ran, his long legs popping him up like a cork. He was one of the many foals bred on Mr. F. O. Davis's Morgan Horse farm in Windsor. His sire was Upway Ben Don, Vermont Champion Morgan Stallion, his dam a Saddlebred whose name might have been Jane Doe for all the credit she was given. This union did not produce the show-worthy animal Mr. Davis had hoped for, so he agreed to sell the eight-month-old colt to my father. The two men had met on the horse show circuit when Paul and I were competing, and Daddy had painted a portrait of Mr. Davis's champion stallion with Upway farm in the background.

The fact that Corky was much too young to train or ride was overlooked. He was the baby of the family and doted on accordingly. Who could resist the eager curiosity of that soft, black nose snuffling for treats, the shiny bay coat, silky black mane and luxurious tail, or those luminous brown eyes with their outrageously thick lashes? We were smitten. The little stallion joined our dappled gray mare, Jill, in the barn, with his own spacious box stall. Jill put up with a woman's lot, patiently standing in her straight stall.

We'd had him for a few months when one winter day he began to cough—and cough and cough. My father got the vet over from Manchester. Dr. Treat diagnosed colic and left a large container of a thick, red fluid to be given every few hours. Though I was only ten, my father and I were the in-house veterinary team, a partnership resulting from our shared love of animals. My job this time was to hold Corky's nose straight up—he was still on his feet—while my father pumped the red liquid down his throat from a large syringe. It took my two hands stretched overhead to hold him. Corky was an unwilling patient. He'd shake his head and the thick goo would dribble onto my hands and arms, and even into my hair. I was allowed to stay up later than usual to help with the last dose. When we were done, Corky lay down on the clean sawdust and was still. I was afraid. A horse that "goes down" often never gets up. I wanted to stay with him all night, so he couldn't slip away. Finally my father took my hand.

"That's all we can do. He'll either be alive in the morning or he won't." I knew that despite this flat statement, he was as worried as I was.

I don't know how I slept that night. I do remember clenching my hands and repeating, "Oh please, oh please, oh please," as I drifted off.

The next morning I woke early and threw on the clothes I had flung over the chair. I crept down the stairs, and padded through the living room and kitchen and out the back door, shutting it softly. The barn was a few short steps down from the terrace. I slid the big red door back and slowly walked through the grain room, opening the door into the stall area. Silence filled the barn. Jill's big dark eyes peered over her stall as I passed on the way to Corky's, in a separate room at the end of the short corridor. Still no sound. Usually our boy could be heard whickering in anticipation of a visit and food. Not this morning. As I turned into his stall room, I hardly dared look, but I did. No shiny brown head and cocked ears, no welcoming sound. I hesitated, then called his name softly. Nothing. Again. Nothing.

As a wave of nausea and grief began to rise in me, there was a sound of scrambling. In a few seconds, there he was, all horsey smiles, pushing his nose against my hand. I hugged his head, crying and laughing, then unbolted the stall door, ran in, and threw my arms around his neck, burying my face in his mane.

I raced into the house to tell my father, who got up and out to the barn in record time. Corky was corky, as if he'd never been sick. I opened the feed bin and dug the scoop into his breakfast oats.

Not So Hot Lunch

Steam rose from huge aluminum pots on the Tappan six-burner donated to our school. A fishy smell permeated the basement room housing the kitchen and dining areas. Now in the sixth grade, I was a part of the rotating crew of students excused early to help set tables, serve, and clean up after hot lunch. Being part of the team made us feel mature and important, and most days I looked forward to my duty, but as I entered the room that day, I knew I would hate it. As fumes invaded my nostrils, I knew it would be another day of force feeding, of stern supervision while everyone cleaned their plates or else.

The cook came out of the kitchen area, wiping her hands on her big white apron, its starched expanse emphasizing her ample figure. Wire-rimmed glasses fogged above her steam-reddened cheeks.

"Hi, girls. Start with salt and peppers, then the silver—and make sure you set it straight."

Mrs. Ada Herschberg came every day to prepare a well-rounded lunch, the only good meal some kids got. She made six dollars a day according to Edith Wiley, the local columnist, and earned every penny. A typical lunch might involve mashing countless potatoes, making multiple meat loaves with gravy, and overcooking pounds of string beans. Her daughter, Ina, who looked like Lil' Abner's beautiful Daisy Mae in conservative dress, usually came to help in the kitchen. She smiled at us a lot and we basked in the glow—everyone had a crush on Ina, who at eighteen was to us the epitome of glamour and sophistication.

There were always a couple of parents on duty, marshaling the troops into some form of coordinated action. During lunch they and the teachers sat at the tables as monitors. Our teacher and principal, Mrs. Winfield, sat with the upper grades, so I was under her beady eye.

"There are those who must do without. We must be grateful for every bite," she said if she saw us pushing food around. Usually the meals were fairly tasty, so we didn't often do it, but that day's dish was, for me, in a class by itself.

I held my breath and averted my eyes as I served the warm, laden plates. Today's main dish, Salmon Pea Wiggle, was a dietician's revenge, healthy but revolting. Cream sauce oozing over limp toast like a melting glacier, punctuated with both pale pink and green lumps, it was a concoction surely invented by someone who loathed children. Resembling wallpaper paste in looks and consistency, its potent odor triggered my gag reflex before the first bite. Having to serve myself the dreaded dish was the ultimate indignity.

When everyone was served and helpers seated, Mrs. Winfield folded her hands over her formidable bosom, swathed in purple that day.

"Let us pray."

As we joined in thanking the Deity, my eye slits watched the plate in front of me. The specialty of the day lay there insolently, cooling to glue and flaunting a side of beets. After the Amen, those of us with discerning palates—and who ate breakfast daily—were reluctantly poking at the dish when a voice broke the silence.

"Hey, look at this."

Carl was known for clowning around and causing what Mrs. Winfield called "disruptions," but we thought he was hilarious. Now he used his fork like a palette knife, spreading beets into the signature dish, turning it cotton candy pink. Laughing, most of us followed suit.

Mrs. Winfield's bosom heaved with indignation. She invoked her *I will not tolerate* mantra, this time about playing with food, but we had lost all reason and forgotten what could result from flagrant disobedience.

"Look at mine," came a shout from down the table.

"I made swirls!" said Carole.

We were inspired, unwittingly channeling the spirit of Expressionism, creating little Jackson-Pollocks-on-a-Plate. George lobbed a forkful at Carl. Patty tipped her plate so soggy toast and pink paste could ooze over the plate's edge and onto the oilcloth. Dali would have loved it. I was more restrained, sitting two seats from the outrage at the head of the table, but managed a pastel homage to Van Gogh.

Mrs. Winfield rose, her face now almost the color of her bosom.

"You will all report to my office after lunch!" she said, pointing an indignant finger at each budding artist. She hesitated. "No, you will go now, you ungrateful children. Now!"

The sound of picnic benches scraping back was accompanied by the giggles of leftover hysteria. The table looked like a Sherwin Williams nightmare.

All eyes followed the march to the door. Daisy Mae wasn't smiling now, but I thought I saw a wink. As we mounted the stairs, Mrs. Winfield was the only thing still steaming, pronouncing us incorrigible and worse, until she needed all her breath to get to the top. Because so many of us had misbehaved, we trusted the punishment wouldn't be severe, and, most wonderfully, knew we wouldn't have to finish our lunch.

Back in the classroom—her tiny office was too small for all us—we kept our eyes on our desks and our mouths from smiling. As our punishment was pronounced, our faces were pitiful.

My essay on the dire need of starving children all over the world was no less than epic.

The Doctor Was In

Clip, clop, swish. Our horses' hooves kicked last fall's leaves, still thick on the woodland path. It was unusually warm for a June day in Vermont, so I wore only a sleeveless shirt with my dungarees. Paul and I were on one of our day jaunts, exploring an old stagecoach trail that Daddy had found on an ancient map. Several miles along the ancient trail, we came to an impasse caused by severe erosion—dislodged rocks were piled precariously on an uphill grade. It was awe-inspiring to think that stagecoaches could have negotiated even a new trail in this terrain. Although we couldn't cover the entire length of the trail, we were happy to have found and explored at least part of it. We headed home.

"Let's trot!" Paul called back. I gave a little kick to Jill, my rotund dappled gray, and she stepped out smartly. The path was straight there, allowing me to gaze off into the trees. The sun's rays piercing the woods with golden shafts reminded me of some of the paintings in my parents' art books.

I felt Jill's front legs going down. *How could she go down on a solid path?* In a second I realized she must have slipped through a stone culvert, a very shallow one, since the openings on either side didn't show. With the old leaf cover, there had been no sign of danger.

Broken legs! As my mind formed this image and its probable outcome, I too was falling, Jill's lurch having pitched me off to the right. I didn't think to position myself properly, arms around head, as I looked back to see what had happened to my beloved pet. I landed, sat up and, to my amazement, saw her pull herself up and stand firmly, quietly waiting for me to remount.

"Good Jillybeans!" Sighing with relief, I stood up and went to her. Then I noticed Paul. He had come back and dismounted. He stared at my right side, saying nothing. I looked down. Shock—my right hand hung just below the elbow joint. There was a large lump under my skin near the shoulder. Between hand and shoulder was a bulging straight ridge, the skin stretched tight and thin. My elbow had popped out of its socket from the weight on my outstretched arm, forcing the forearm up to the shoulder.

"AAAH!" The sight made me forget I was the brave girl who picked herself up and got right back on when thrown. My first shriek was my last, though, because Paul walked quickly up to me, grabbed my hand between his two, and jerked down, hard. My elbow slid smoothly back into place. I stopped wailing, though I was still upset and shaky.

Then, how to get me back on without the use of my dangling right arm? This had not been covered in my riding lessons. At this point, our family owned only Jill and Corky, so Paul's horse was a summer rental.

Our two mounts were not yet well acquainted and not in the mood for becoming so. Every time Paul held my foot and pushed me up, Mischief, true to his name, nipped at Jill and danced away, straining his reins in Paul's grip. Jill nipped back, offended by this Johnny-Come-Lately, their jostling throwing me off balance. The whole operation would be defeated and we'd have to start again. Paul would push me up, while I would try to grab the saddle with my left hand, the one holding the reins, to steady myself enough to throw my leg over. The first few times I was unsuccessful and almost went completely over the saddle and down the other side. By the time I was at long last astride, we were sweaty and exhausted. I must have been still in shock, because I didn't think about what that useless arm could mean. Paul rode close by my side for the few miles home, the beasts having finally settled down, except for occasional teeth baring.

When we arrived in the front yard, Mom stepped down from the terrace, smiling.

"Did you have a good ride?" She hadn't noticed my inert limb yet. I gave her a full account of the accident, not sparing the gruesome details. She remained calm. *Didn't she get it?* She helped me dismount and led me into the kitchen, where she soaked my elbow alternately in bowls of warm and cold water, then put my arm in a dish towel sling. I was sure our next stop would be Dr. Pingree's office, but no. I wore that sling for a week, until my arm gradually regained strength and

45

movement. Despite the healing, I recall being secretly offended that Mom hadn't taken my injury more seriously.

What I didn't appreciate until much later was that I had already been seen and treated by a perfectly competent person, my twelve-year-old brother.

Our House, 1941

Paul, Mark, Mom, Jeanne and Daddy

Landman's Hardware
on the Square

Third grade
Age 8

With Paul, riding Jill and Ceci at home

In show attire
Age 9

Snowdrop greets
a dinner guest.

Mark astride a
reluctant Ramsey

Age 10, with grownup Snowdrop and one of the Tweedles

Good weather for Flexible Flyers

Daddy, Paul, Little Red Squeak, and latest Chevy

With Mark and my
new-braces smile.
Age 12

Thub Rawson haying

With Mark and Corky

Winter at One Derry Lane

Mom, holding
new puppy's leash

Ever-dapper Daddy

Paul with Flicka

The Dream

Daybreak. Winter.

Compact as a ship's cabin, my room was just big enough for the narrow bed, white bureau, and small bookcase against the wall by the doorway. It was spare, except for a mirror and the large print of Bellows' "Lady Jeanne." I loved the wide window over my bed, framing the valley view.

Except when I had the dream.

Most mornings, when I poked my head out of the covers, the frost on the window made shapes like starbursts, or flowers, even birds. I ran my thumb across the panes, collecting frost under my nail, adding flourishes to the designs subzero temperatures had created. When I woke after a night with the dream, the frost patterns were fingers, clawed and menacing. Until I realized, *It's not true! It was just a bad dream!* Relief washed over me. I threw off the covers, and raced to stand on the warm grate in the hall. I could hear my father downstairs, poking the coals in the fireplace and throwing on new logs. Bacon was frying in the kitchen. My brothers shoved, trying to get on the grate, too. Life was back to normal.

I had the dream only a few times, but each time I woke to see those icy fingers splayed against the panes. Always, relief came quickly. *It isn't true!* It was a bad dream, nothing to worry about. The frost patterns again became starbursts, flowers, birds.

I had the dream one last time after that March day a few years later. As I woke and began my litany of self-reassurance, reality exploded into my consciousness, *It's true—this time, true.*

Maybe the dream had been telling me.

Could a young girl's dreams make it happen?

The Liar's Accomplice

Mark ran, staying just ahead of me, as we circled the first floor. Past the wing chair, the fireplace, the sofa, Daddy's reading chair, the banjo clock and the rocker, through the front hall, between the sofa and Mom's desk in the sitting room, barely missing the four-poster in the guest room, down the back hallway, and into the living room again. As he careened just out of reach, he smirked back at me. I wanted to kill the little monster.

At nine and twelve, my brother and I still fought like wildcats. The last time he really did hurt me. We were throwing things from behind barricades of sofa cushions when I turned around after grabbing more ammo. The timing was perfect—his, that is. *The Last of the Mohicans* hit me squarely in the mouth, causing my new braces to shred the inside of my upper lip. He looked chagrined, but didn't apologize. I was too upset to continue our battle.

One day soon after, we were in the house alone when hostilities broke out again. I don't remember why; it didn't take much to set us off. As we raced around the house, my mouth still sore, I was intent on revenge.

On the third lap, my eye caught sight of his beloved Gene Autry boots lying beside the rocking chair. I grabbed one and hurled it. To my astonishment, the boot caught him in the back of the head and laid open a gash worthy of a Frankenstein movie. Blood spurted from the wound, running between the small fingers clutching his head.

"Oh, Markie, I'm sorry! I didn't mean to do it!"

Of course I did, but hadn't anticipated the damage I might do. I got washcloths and water and mopped at the wound as he sat on the floor in a daze. By the time the spurting slowed to an ooze, we looked like a couple of crime victims and the floor was a slippery crimson.

As we cleaned up, we began to contemplate our parent's reaction when they got home. They didn't often deliver corporal punishment, but *the look* from Mom could shrivel a boa constrictor, not to mention any of the onerous sentences she might impose. Plus, knowing I'd nearly killed him and that I'd be revealed for the monster *I* could be, made me quake even more.

"I'll tell them I slipped and hit my head on the rocker," said Mark. He was willing to lie? For me? Weak sister that I was, I jumped at his offer.

A few minutes later, the car crunched down the driveway. Daddy got out and went to his studio.

"What happened?" asked Mom, giving us her *have-you-two-been-at-it-again* look.

"We were running and I fell and hit my head on the end of the rocker," said Mark. I watched in awe at his smooth delivery. My mother looked at him, then at me. I nodded and looked down.

"Well, you kids are going to have to give up this fighting. You're too old to be chasing each other around. Next time, something worse could happen."

It worked. I was relieved, grateful to Mark, and had new appreciation for my little brother's loyalty. I don't think I would have been as magnanimous. Mom patched up Mark's head and things got back to normal.

Though it bled profusely, the wound wasn't deep. But there would be a visible scar for some time.

The afternoon passed and so did my relief. With every tick of the banjo clock, my guilt magnified. Mark had gone upstairs to play in his room. I opened *Little Women*, but read the same page six times. I got out my Katie Keene paper doll, to design a new evening dress, something I usually found absorbing. This time it didn't work. Every time Mom passed through the room, I expected her to say, "What *really* happened?" I knew I'd confess. She didn't. It was torture, worse than any punishment she might have devised.

Finally I could bear it no more. With an aching stomach, pounding heart, and clammy palms, I shuffled into the kitchen. I stood, picking at the hem of my tee shirt.

"I did it." I kept my eyes on the floor, lest I get *the look*.

She waited, saying nothing. More torture. I burst into tears and told her the whole story.

"I thought as much."

Still weeping, I promised I would never do anything like that again. Or lie. Ha.

The incident didn't end our battles, but no more projectiles were used. Within a year, I was far too superior for such nonsense, instead asking Mom in a pained voice, "Can't you *do* something about that child?"

But I had learned that when the chips were down, the little guy who could make dents in my shins with his hard shoes would stand with me.

WHOA!

Paul and I were nearing the end of one of our long trail rides. This time I rode Corky, now three years old. Inexperienced, he nonetheless took to new adventures easily, showing an even temperament. The next half hour would be the test of that.

Paul spoke. "It's getting dark. We'd better stop at Elmer's and ask him to call Mom."

We had almost covered the three miles down from Londonderry. The road wound along the West River, past the Cool Edge Laundry in someone's garage, the Luinetti's farmhouse, and the Wadleigh's cottage, perched above the summer wetlands. As we rounded the last bend before town, a decrepit rail car with a rounded roof and a rear platform came into view. It was a relic of the defunct West River Railroad and sat alone on a brushy piece of prime property overlooking the river. It was home to Finnie Hoy, a former railroad man, as reflected by his crusty overalls and the engineer's cap squashed over his brow. Everyone knew Finnie. He had stoked fires on the locomotives until the last one puffed into town. How he commandeered that caboose was a mystery, but its comforts were apparently more than just physical for him—he was rarely away from it.

As usual, Finnie sat on what passed for his front steps, keeping track of comings and goings. He always waved and seemed friendly, aided perhaps by the ever-present bottle of Jim Beam. His nose resembled an overripe eggplant, the rest of his face doughy and pockmarked. Like any small town, ours had its characters.

As we clopped past at a walk, he waved. Then, "Whoa!" This was new. Usually he said nothing. We returned the wave, but that didn't seem to satisfy Finnie. Heaving himself to his feet, lurching heavily, he began to lumber toward us. The first hint of anxiety prickled the back of my neck.

"Whoa! Whoa!"

We smiled and waved again, kicking up to a trot until we were out of his sight, then slowing to a walk as we entered the village. Minutes later we were tying our reins to the rail outside the post office behind Elmer's Market when Finnie's raggedy figure loomed out of the dusk. How did he get there so quickly? As he drew closer, now within a couple of feet of me, the prickle was replaced with real fear. It was one thing to see him waving from his front stoop, another to have his florid face close and to smell his breath, curdling the air with each cry. He seized Corky's tail in both hands and sat back, almost to the ground. What was he *thinking?* That this was a runaway horse? Maybe he thought he was saving me. Corky was used to having his tail held and pulled with brushing, but having full body weight on it was another thing. Amazingly, he didn't kick, though he strained his head around, ears up, taking in this new development. I patted him and made soothing sounds, at the same time keeping a wary eye on Finnie. I had never been near someone who was drunk and it was terrifying. He was focused on that tail, but I feared his attention might turn to me.

"Whoa!" he shouted. He was now seated on the ground, but still maintained his grip on Corky's long black tail.

"We'd better not leave 'em here," said Paul, his voice quiet and even. His calm helped me control my fear. Untying the reins, we led our mounts around to the front of the store, me in the lead. Finnie stumbled along, Corky's tail still wound about his fingers. I could hardly breathe. On the sidewalk in front of the store, I was still too far away to be heard inside. Stretching Corky's reins to the limit, I mounted the shallow steps and crossed the landing, just managing to push open the screen door. Ever curious, he followed me, mounting the steps and poking his muzzle over my shoulder. Charlie Pearson, a man of dry humor, occupied a stool at the soda fountain. He swiveled and, not missing a beat, quipped,

"Come on in. 'Lot of other jackasses come in heah."

Jackass? Any other time, I would have been hurt—no, mad—but now there were more pressing concerns.

"Elmer, can you call Mom and tell her we're almost home? And Finnie's..."

"Sure thing. You okay?"

Elmer's shock of black hair and engaging grin appeared from behind the Wonder Bread display. The sound of Finnie's cries caught the two men's attention. Charlie set down his A&W and came to the door. Stepping outside, with a "Come on now, Fin," he detached Finnie, who was now seated on the landing at Corky's rear, tail gripped, still whoa-ing. Grabbing him like a sack of grain, Charlie heaved Finnie into his Jeep.

"I'll call your mother—you two get going," said Elmer. His kind voice and the departure of Finnie reassured me.

"Thanks, Elmer, we will."

Charlie's Jeep zipped ahead of us across the bridge and turned left down the dip, where he deposited Finnie in front of the Farmers Exchange. There was no danger of his making it up the rise to the road for a good while. Following at a brisk pace, we called our thanks to Charlie as we turned to go up river. Finnie's bellow followed us, growing gradually fainter until there was quiet except for the hollow ring of hooves on hard-packed dirt.

No doubt Finnie eventually managed to trudge home to his cozy caboose and the familiar solace of Jim Beam. It was long time before we rode by his place again. I liked to think his soggy mind held only good intentions, but was thankful I wasn't alone.

Magic Not So Black

The boggy area down behind our house was an unattractive blot on the view from the rear windows and terrace. Beyond the weedy swamp, the land rose on the other side to the whitewashed oval of our riding ring. Farther out were the fields, river, and mountain.

My father had heard stories of abundant water sources being found by "water witches" and made an appointment for a "dowsing." I wonder if he would have believed those stories if he had heard them when we were living in the Massachusetts suburbs. Living in the country seems to open the mind to ideas once thought provincial, even fantastic. My father was ready to rely on a magician of sorts to determine whether there was enough water to create the pond we envisioned.

Crickets sang, a wasp buzzed; everything was dry that July day except the bog—it oozed, algae sliming the surface. A dusty, unfamiliar pickup pulled into the parking space near Daddy's studio, and a short, wiry man stepped down. No hooked nose, no pointed hat, no broom, and it was a man. Everyone knew witches were women.

He reached back into the cab and pulled out a thin, forked branch, willow maybe. After a few moments' conversation, he and my father trudged up into the pasture and out of sight.

About twenty minutes later they reappeared, the water witch gripping the forked end of his "wand" in both hands. The dowsing stick was visibly bending, pointed end toward the ground. It appeared to be almost too powerful for him to hold. He continued through the pasture gate, down over the drive, and across the paddock, ending at the bog, where the wand's tip quivered in its effort to reach the ground. My father and the witch talked animatedly, then shook hands.

Within days, a huge backhoe appeared. The operator drove it around to the swampy area and began to scoop enormous shovelfuls of weeds and mud. If it hadn't had tank tracks, it would be there still. After several hours, it had created a hole almost the length of the house and barn together, the excavated dirt dumped around the sides. If this was a mistake, it was going to be a big one.

When the digging was done, the dirt piles were spread out and smoothed into a gentle mound running the whole way around, to be seeded later. Then we waited. Days went by. Like the proverbial watched pot, it seemed forever before anything more than the usual ooze was visible. If anyone was skeptical about eventual success, they didn't say so.

After about a week, we could see a puddle forming at the bottom of the hole. Would this be it? With maddening slowness, the water rose, finally to the point where we knew my father's faith in the witch had been justified. My mother expressed hers by buying a few goldfish, which she deposited to "add color." The eight or ten bowl-sized guppies expressed theirs by reproducing at a prodigious rate, their offspring eventually morphing into pond-size creatures in shades from orange to a speckled white.

Now the view from the rear of the house was perfect; sparkling pond, riding ring, rolling fields, trees, river, and Glebe Mountain. All thanks to a good witch's magic.

Sex for the Beginner

"What's that?"

I tried to sound casual as I responded to my friend Ginny's tale of a rape in her village.

"It's what your father does to your mother," Ginny said.

"Oh yeah." I tried to sound nonchalant. What my father did to my mother? I didn't know my father did *anything* to my mother.

Ginny and I had been out riding, but had dismounted to rest on the schoolhouse steps. Her declaration brought my to my feet.

"Oh my gosh—I just remembered I'm supposed to home in ten minutes!"

My horse and I arrived home in a lather, she with sweat, I with anticipation.

Bursting into the kitchen, I found my mother preparing Friday's baked beans and brown bread. Without preamble, I blurted,

"What's rape?"

My mother paused, spoon in midair, then replied,

"We'll talk about that later."

Mom's voice had her *and that's that* tone. Chastened, I left the room. Within twenty-four hours, however, having traveled with dispatch the fourteen miles to the big library in Manchester, Mom settled me on the sofa with several volumes of sex education for young people. She did not suggest we talk later about what I was about to read.

I began. The information was barely credible and used terms completely new to me. There was one constant, "See Glossary." I flipped back and forth until my mind was spinning, each time learning another portent-laden word. Read and check glossary, read and check glossary. I emerged from my studies an hour or so later, dazed, amazed, and certain of only one thing—the meaning of "Glossary."

Mrs. Geddes Gets the Message

To some believers, signs are given, like the Virgin Mary's image appearing in a fried egg sandwich or the sudden "bleeding" from the hand of a roadside statue. The truly devout believe these are ignored at their peril. A sign came to one believer at a particularly fortunate time for me.

I was one of those kids who seized the "opportunity" to sell magazine subscriptions that summer. One particularly hot day, after fruitless visits to several farms, the opportunity seemed more like a sentence. My final stop was the Tuttle's.

I stood in the road, staring at the door. I wanted to skip that house; I *really* wanted to skip that house, because I knew I would find Mrs. Geddes there. She was housekeeper for the three bachelor brothers on the farm next to ours. I had always been a little afraid of her, with her pinched face and dour expression, but I hadn't made a sale all day. I marched up to the house and knocked. When she appeared and didn't slam the door, I began my pitch. Soon things were looking up. She was about to sign on the dotted line for a year's subscription to *The Catholic Digest* when she balked.

"I don't know. My subscription to *The Christian Herald* isn't up yet. I'll have to think about it."

I mumbled something about getting back to her and turned away. The door closed behind me, the lock clicked. When I reached the road, I turned and gazed back at the house, the sweet taste of the sale souring in my mouth. I started back toward the door, stopped, and turned away. I couldn't face that dried-up-apple of a woman again. Dejected and sweaty, I plodded home.

I whined as my mother handed me a lemonade.

"Mrs. Geddes says she'll think about it. That means *no*."

"Not necessarily. She may change her mind."

I was not to be soothed and slumped face down on the sofa.

Crack! A bolt of lightning shook the house. More bolts pierced the murky sky. Thunder roared, and rain fell as if God were dumping his washbowl. It was a typical Vermont summer storm, wild and loud, better than the Fourth of July fireworks. When the show was over, sun would sweep the meadow, a rainbow might rise over the river, and puddles in the driveway would beckon waders. Those storms were scary, too, and this storm was especially violent. I was glad to be inside.

At the post office the next morning, everyone was agog with the news. Lightning had struck the Tuttles' house the afternoon before.

"Blew the kitchen sink clear 'crost the room!" marveled Thub Rawson. Fortunately, Mrs. G was upstairs at the time.

Later that day, the party line sounded our ring, two longs and a short. I picked up.

"Hello, Jeanne? This is Mrs. Geddes. I'll take that subscription after all."

Mrs. Geddes knew a sign when she saw one.

False Hopes

There were several cans of tennis balls lying around, though no one in the family played. However, they did come in handy one August day.

The Bennetts came for a picnic, bringing their daughter Sally and her friend visiting from Massachusetts. Both girls were my brother Paul's age, almost fifteen. I was twelve. Right away I noticed that we three wore identical outfits, white tee shirts and blue denims, but it took only a few seconds more to notice a big difference. Their clothes graced tall and shapely bodies, while my rolled-up Levis depended heavily on my tooled leather belt to stay up and my Fruit of the Loom tee shirt graced absolutely nothing. As I gazed at them, I burned with envy and longed for age and curves.

We had a cookout: hot dogs, hamburgers, corn, even toasted marshmallows. With my brothers, the girls and I played badminton on the lawn, went to the paddock to pet the horses, and inspected the new goldfish in the pond. Sally and her friend were fun. My envy receded to a dull green.

"Goodbye, goodbye! Come again soon!"

Their black Ford pulled away, whitewalls gleaming as they spun down the drive. We waved until they were out of sight. My parents went into the house, Paul and Mark resumed badminton, and I wandered down to the barn, my favorite place to spend time.

As I walked through the storeroom, I noticed a box of tennis balls in the corner. A thought struck me. I grabbed the box, pulled off the lid, and took out one fuzzy yellow ball. Running into the house, I grabbed a knife from the kitchen drawer, and sped back to the barn. After laboring for several minutes, I crept back into the house and up to my room. After listening to be sure my nosey brothers weren't coming, I completed my work and turned, boldly facing the mirror. Under my tee shirt, were two yellow bumps. Showing faintly through on one side, *Spalding*—on the other, three dots.

Sighing, I removed my fuzzy falsies. Maybe someday...

Transformed

My mother was at the cutting board, chopping vegetables. I sat on the high stool, kneading the yellow into the oleomargarine. The chopping grew faster. I was checking for stray bits of color capsule when she spoke.

"Kay has badly disappointed her family."

Kay was the granddaughter of friends of the family. She lived in Ohio, but visited at least once a summer. My mother admired her enormously, praising her often and extravagantly. Kay was everything I was not and wished to be: older, tan, curvaceous, and clever. Her visits always threw me into paroxysms of envy. To hear my mother utter those words now was shocking.

"Why?"

"Because she's pregnant! Her fiancé has had to drop out of the Coast Guard Academy to marry her. That little hot pants! If that ever happens to you, I'll help you, but don't expect me to sympathize."

Huh? Me? If that ever happened to me? I had just reached puberty, never had a date, and only sketchily understood the process for getting pregnant. Yet already I was guilty, scorned, and warned. I felt as if I'd been punched. Here was the naming of the nameless fear I carried: my mother lacked faith in me.

"It's disgraceful. After all her family has done for her, to behave in such a shameless fashion. She's just a little tart!"

Transformed. In the minute it took her to learn of Kay's transgression, *that wonderful girl* had become *that little hot pants*, a reverse metamorphosis, butterfly to pupa.

The fall from grace can be so quick. Once esteemed, suddenly reviled; no compassion, no forgiveness—and my position was already precarious.

"What will they do?"

"I have no idea. Of course *his* life is ruined."

I looked at the margarine bag, limp in my hands. The color was perfect—or so it seemed.

Sacrificial Lambs

The school bus jeep dropped us off. My brothers and I straggled home down the lane, the few fallen leaves whispering under our feet. After peanut butter cookies and milk, I went out to visit the animals: horses dozing in the paddock, chickens clucking in the coop, ducks gliding on the pond, geese waddling about giving me the beady eye, and lambs...where were the lambs?

Wooly ellipses with pointy faces and airplane-wing ears, our Shropshires made up in cuteness what they lacked in brains. We named them Tweedledum and Tweedledee.

My father sat us down soon after he bought them in May.

"Now kids, we're running a farm, which means raising our own food. These lambs are part of that. So one day in October, when you come home from school, they won't be here and I don't want to hear anything about it." He explained that a man would pick them up and deliver them to the freeze locker in Chester.

"Do you understand?" He had warned us before that we would be raising animals for food, and that it was the only way we could make a go of living in the country. Because he was such an animal lover, I doubted he could go through with slaughtering ours.

"Yes, Daddy," we said, but I couldn't imagine it. I knew it was the fate of some of our poultry, but who could kill these sweet little creatures with their tiny, nibbling lips and plaintive little baas? Fall was months away; things could change.

As summer passed, the twins grew roly-poly on grass and grain, but in late July, Tweedledum got sick. An unnoticed cut on his leg became infected, creating a grisly, maggot-infested wound. We feared he would die. Following the vet's instructions, Daddy dipped the leg twice a day in a special wash. It healed. Our fat little man lived.

Now the roly-polys were nowhere in sight. I checked the barn, surveyed the field.

Then I remembered. It was October.

In May, I'd said I understood. Now I truly did. Everyone on the farm had a job—even the worms Mom ordered for the compost pit—and the job of most creatures was to eat and be eaten. My eyes teared. I pictured my father surrendering the lambs and knew it had been hard. He saved Dum's life, after all. Was this how real farmers felt, having to kill animals so tenderly cared for? Did sacrificing them to provide for their families make it less painful?

I remembered their little faces with the shoe-button eyes, their shiny black hooves, those jutting ears, the way they let Mark ride them, clinging to their wool. By just being and baa-ing, they added to our small farm family.

My sensitive parents waited months to serve the inevitable Sunday dinner. Mom brought on the steaming platter: leg of lamb, beautifully browned, with a wonderful aroma and surrounded by roasted potatoes. I'd always loved lamb, crispy fat and all. Now I wondered whether it was Dee or Dum. I looked around the table. All eyes were averted. Daddy carved with great deliberation, filled the plates, and passed them around.

"Nice job cleaning the garage, Paul."

Mom agreed. "Yes, very. Have some peas. Gravy? When will the wood be delivered, Walt?"

I understood. We were real farmers now. I picked up my fork.

"May I please have the mint jelly?"

Winter Black

Early one morning of a later October, my mother called me into their bedroom after Daddy had gone downstairs. I was thirteen. The night before, she and my father had returned from a trip to a Boston doctor. Daddy was having pain in his back. Mrs. Van Atten had come down the lane to be with Mark and me. Paul was away at school. It was dark when they came in.

"Hi, how did it go?" Looking up from our Canasta game, Mrs. Van Atten's voice was light, which didn't fool anybody. Uncharacteristically, Daddy said nothing, just hung up his coat and hat and went upstairs.

"As well as can be expected." Mom tried to sound light, too, but her voice was strained. The subject was dropped.

Now, as she settled me beside her on the edge of the bed, I again felt the tension of the previous night.

"I have something to tell you," she said. "Daddy has a little growth in his stomach that has to be removed. He'll have an operation at Mass General next week." My own stomach turned to lead.

Daddy and I had become closer since we moved to Vermont. He was around more, read to us in the evenings, shared my love of the animals, and had time to play badminton, Ping-Pong, and "Catch." Along with an Irish temper, he brought a lively humor and energy to the household, a foil for Mom's restrained and serious temperament. I remember the morning he came down to breakfast and wrapped his arms around her, saying, "Look at this kids!" Picking her up away from her pancake griddle, he swung her around. She looked embarrassed, but pleased. Life was good.

I have no idea what I said or asked that morning. I remember only fear. The idea of Daddy's being sick was not credible. He was never sick.

During the next three months, Paul studied and marched at his military school, coping as best he could, far from home. I don't think Mom called him often, long distance calls being expensive and she not being naturally communicative. I believe her idea was the less we knew, the less we'd worry.

"As well as can be expected." That or a variation of it was the only report Mom offered when she came home from the hospital in Springfield, where Daddy was transferred after his operation. He had a horror of hospitals, even refusing to visit me during the several days I was hospitalized for a tonsillectomy the previous July.

Mom made the fifty-four mile round trip alone almost every day. Hospital rules prevented anyone under sixteen from visiting. She was told right away that he would not survive, so knew she faced a future raising three children alone. I didn't know that then and didn't think of her, only of the tight knot in my stomach, the fear of asking, and the frustration of feeling excluded. I wrote letters to Daddy and got a couple of brief replies, then nothing. His illness had reduced his bold, go-ahead script to a tentative scrawl.

Now it was my job to feed the horses and clean their stalls before going to school. It was tough work when the night temperatures dropped below freezing. Bringing wood in was another of my chores—with a stove and a fireplace, we burned several cords each winter.

Mom still got up early, cooked, cleaned, washed, ironed, shopped, paid bills, built fires, filled the kerosene heaters, shoveled snow, all the while making that daily trip. I think she took a leave from her job. She later said she and my father never discussed his prognosis, denying themselves some comfort in facing his impending death together.

We slogged through the rest of October, November, and into December. Then, joy—Daddy came home for Christmas. He was thin, but smiling, happy to be home. Paul was back and helped Mom put up the tree. Mark and I threw the usual globs of tinsel at it. My friend Carole's parents invited us for Christmas dinner. The festive table and lively chatter brought a feeling of normalcy that had been missing for so long. Daddy seemed his old self, telling stories, laughing, eating.

Within a day, the situation had reversed. Daddy stayed in bed, in terrible pain, his cries filling the stairway, penetrating the living room door, pouring through the heat vents. When we crept up to our bedrooms, trying not to make the stairs creak, he heard the slightest noise, yelling, "Keep it down!" I was terrified, by his anger, by the thought of what might happen.

A few days later, he came downstairs and lay on the living room sofa by the fire. I thought he felt better, but soon he began to groan and hold his stomach. Mom asked Mark and me to leave the room. Mark went upstairs, I to the sitting room across the hall. Although both doors were shut, I could hear him.

"Connie, I'm going to die!" Her murmurs were inaudible.

I don't know how long it was before I heard the slap of chains rolling over snow. Looking out, I saw a long, white vehicle with a red cross on the side. It had come for Daddy. Neither Mark nor I was called to say goodbye, and I was afraid to venture out from my banishment. As the ambulance pulled away, I crouched on the floor, clenching my hands beside my forehead as it touched the rug. Again I prayed, "Oh please, oh please, oh please."

My prayer seemed to be answered. An operation relieved the adhesions causing the pain. I thought this would let him come home, but it didn't. January and February passed. Still no word of his returning to us.

At the beginning of March, I wrote another letter and enclosed my latest school picture, hoping it would cheer him up. Mom had already left for the hospital, so to get it in that day's mail, I would have had to walk to town and back, more than two miles. I didn't go, blaming the cold. My letter was mailed the next day.

In the three a.m. blackness of March ninth, I was jangled awake by our ring. I ran down to answer.

"Mrs. Heffron? May I speak to Mrs. Heffron?" Mom was right behind me. I handed the phone to her.

"What shall I do? What shall I do?" Though she'd long known she'd get this call, it was as if it was unexpected. After a few moments, she placed the receiver back on its hook and slumped into Daddy's reading chair. I climbed into her lap, something I hadn't done since I was a toddler. I wanted to comfort her; I assured her I would not die. A wandering conversation got us through until dawn. We didn't cry. When it began to be light, she went up to Mark's room to tell him. I never heard or saw him cry either.

The next day, Paul arrived by bus in Manchester. He got into the car, looking handsome and serious in his uniform. I held my breath as Mom told him. Brimming with tears, I knew that now we would all cry together. Paul sat quietly, then said, "Oh," and again, "Oh." With great difficulty, I gulped back my tears; I sensed Mark was doing the same.

We drove home in silence.

That night our grief spilled out in inappropriate ways. We horsed around, shrieking and laughing, until Mom cried out, "Stop that! You have your whole lives ahead of you. Mine is over!"

A few days later, my letter was returned, marked *Undeliverable.*

Aftermath

My father committed the crime of dying. Had he been a murderer packed off to prison, there would have been no less mention of him. "I can't bear it," my mother said. So I took refuge in the barn.

As I groomed the horses, the thin skin of my composure split. Each stroke of the curry brush brought a cry of rage, and sobs of "Why?" Why?" until I buried my face in a broad, furry neck, quiet at last.

One of those whys was *Why was I left with the one who didn't want me?* Mom was a superb artist, manager, seamstress, and cook, but she had little talent for expressing love. I'd always felt unsure of hers. Still vivid is the moment a few years earlier when she walked by and brushed her hand along my cheek. The feeling of utter surprise and joy is unforgettable. It's the only time I remember her showing me spontaneous affection. When Daddy died, it was like being left alone in a cold, bare room.

We didn't go to school for a week. Mom and Paul went to Massachusetts for the rituals my grandparents wanted. Mark and I were deemed too young, so a friend came to stay. Mom hated everything about those few days, the drinking and boisterous laughter at the Irish wake, the impersonal Catholic funeral, especially that her husband was buried in a forsaken corner of the cemetery, being "fallen." I wondered how could she have left him there, alone in the cold too. Years later, she told me that his parents said Daddy's death was God's punishment for having married outside the church. A wrathful God could strike down good people, ruin lives. I was furious. Hadn't she been furious too?

At home after the funeral, my brothers followed my mother's stoic lead, at least when I was around. To look at us, you wouldn't have guessed a tragedy occurred. Mom dropped us off at the ski slopes most days. My brothers were ski racers and went off to practice. My chronically cold hands and feet kept me rotating between the slopes and the lodge, alone. There was a sense of nothingness, a blankness that kept emotions at bay.

In my room, I collected all the things Daddy had given me. A box of note cards with a horse's head on the front, the silver and turquoise necklace of Indian symbols, the scarf holder with a tiny, sculpted silver horse attached, the cuff bracelet with my name engraved on it. I didn't use the note cards for several years. It would have felt like sending some of my father away.

My mother decided she couldn't manage another Vermont winter, so made plans to move in early September to her family's big house in Rhode Island, then occupied by only my grandmother. I wonder how Grammy felt about having us. She and my mother were not close, but I'm sure it never occurred to her to refuse.

My brother Paul went back to his school in New York State and Mark and I finished the year at Central Elementary. When summer came, Mom began the sad business of selling off our livestock: chickens, ducks, geese—no dog or cat then—and finally, the horses. My beloved Jill, the dappled gray mare, was sold to a family with three children, who hired me the next summer as a babysitter and riding instructor. I don't remember where our lovely dark bay mare, Ceci, went. Four-year-old Corky, the darling of the family, was sold to another family with children who came with their father to get him. They were thrilled. Other than being proud of Corky, I felt nothing. We had brushed his reddish coat to a high sheen, even braiding ribbons in his black mane, as if he were going into a show. I remember how they fluttered as he was led up the ramp into the van. He turned his head to look back. I raised my hand in a faint wave. Then he was in, the rear gate up and locked. I stood watching until the van disappeared over the rise. As the dust settled, I turned away. There was no reason to stay in Vermont now.

Epilogue

I watch the silt-brown river pound the bridge, dirty spumes exploding upward as water meets cement, then flowing over and beneath with a roar like white sound in Dolby. Just downstream, the floodwater rises to the rear windows of the Green Mountain Farmers Exchange. As the video camera pans left, I see the water washing over the site of the former fire station, obliterated in earlier floods, and across Main Street to the post office behind the now-defunct Elmer's Grocery Store. The road is blocked off with yellow tape, so it's impossible to see what damage lies beyond.

YouTube has brought me from Maryland to South Londonderry in the midst of Hurricane Irene, to witness this latest assault on the place of my childhood home.

After three fires, as many floods, and economic reversals, there isn't much left of the village. The dam and most of the buildings along the West River have been swept away in its seasons of swelling and rage. Taylor's Mill, former home of *insa-outsa an' whirla-whirlas*, is gone too. Landman's Hardware became an upscale food shop, but I hear it folded when its owners closed their restaurant up the hill. Marvin Howard's Brick House-cum-funeral home is still on the corner. There hasn't been a body, at least a dead one, on the premises in years. Though at one time the village's location away from the main highway seemed to be an advantage, over time commerce was lost to

Londonderry, three miles north and more easily reached by tourists and suppliers. My town suffocated from lack of financial oxygen.

Although we moved after my father's death in 1952, my mother kept the house, spending the next seventeen summers there. Our former school jeep driver and postmaster, Orie Slade, and his wife Lena appointed themselves her guardian angels, doing countless thoughtful things without fanfare. After Orie died, my mother remained in touch with Lena and I continued to see her whenever my husband and I visited South 'Derry, until she died at ninety-five.

I've been back many times, first as summer babysitter for the Gannett family in Brattleboro, who bought our Jill; later to visit my mother, with whom I had an amicable, if not close, relationship as an adult. After I married and had a car, during my husband's deployments I drove up to see her and the people and places I'd known so well. It was like slipping into a well-worn glove. In 1966, then the mother of a two-year-old, I stopped to visit with Mrs. Clough, grandmother of my grade school friend Patty. As we sat on the porch watching fishermen in the depleted river, she said, "See them? They won't catch nothin' there, but you can't tell them summah people nothin'." Finally, confirmation that we'd earned acceptance all those years ago, that we weren't "summer people." I was surprised at how good it felt, even then.

During a visit about fifteen years ago, a local friend took me back to my old school, now the Town Clerk's Office, run by one of my younger schoolmates, shy, soft-spoken Jimmy Twitchell. When Jimmy learned who I was, he pushed up his owlish glasses, took one step back and said, "Well, now," his words stretching like molasses. He then disappeared to the back office. I thought that was that, but he soon reappeared to quietly present me with a pint of his own maple syrup. A typical Vermont gesture, understated and kind.

Now, as I keep watching YouTube, the images of destruction recede, replaced by ghosts from the past: Cap Landman in his overalls, counting out ten-penny nails; Curtis Shattuck with his twinkly glasses and kittens; Orie in his jeep or handing out mail and jokes at the post office, and Charlie and Elmer in the grocery store. Even after the TV video ends, those and other images play on, bringing this once lively village back to life. Sixty years have passed since we moved away, but it's evident time will not erase the memories.

My mother reluctantly sold the house in 1969; she found matches in the attic, evidence of games by winter renters' children. She preferred to part with the place rather than chance its being incinerated. The new owners have lovingly maintained it almost as it was, though it is quieter, without animals or children. Though my last months there were sad, it isn't the sadness that lingers, but rather an overall feeling of good fortune for having lived in a world I'd never have known if not for my father's optimistic spirit—and certainly not one my children knew growing up in the Virginia suburbs. He brought the family to a village that has become a touchstone for me, to return to in thought when I feel a shift in my emotional ground. He gave me optimism and a love of people; South Londonderry and its citizens gave me an appreciation of the things I value: simplicity, honesty, kindheartedness, and a sense of humor—not to mention all things rustic. It's hard to find simplicity in today's speed-of-light world, but still possible to find honest, kindhearted, humorous people. Though I'm now a happy transplant in a small, historic city, my Vermont roots have not been severed.

Acknowledgements

When I signed up for a memoir class, I had no thought of writing a book, only of recording a few episodes from my Vermont childhood for my daughters. My teacher, Lynn Schwartz, suggested that there might be a wider audience; I am ever grateful for that and for her invaluable counsel and unflagging encouragement. Laura Oliver, too, has been teacher and supporter; her belief in my writing has been a gift. A special thanks to my dear friend Patsy Helmetag, for her generosity, creativity, and expertise in providing the cover design and final manuscript preparation. Thanks to my husband, Rob, who has encouraged me from the start. Last but not least, thanks to my colleagues in the Broadneck Writers Workshop for offering new ideas and helpful critiques, always kindly, and for their good fellowship along the way.